SCIENCE ENCYCLOPEDIA

SUBSTANCES, MIXTURES AND COMPOUNDS

Om KIDZ

An imprint of Om Books International

Contents

What is a Substance?	4
What is a Mixture?	5
Types of Mixtures	6
Solubility	8
Solid Solution	9
Key Properties of Substances	10
What is a Compound?	12
Classification and Structure of Compounds	13
Organic and Inorganic Compounds	14
Inorganic Compounds	15
Oxides	16
Ores and Minerals	17
Basics of Ions	18
Ionic Structures and their Relevance	19
Process of Ionisation	20
Acids and Bases Fundamentals	22
Lewis Acid and Lewis Bases	23
Neutralisation and Titration	24
The pH and pOH Scales	25
Important Acids	26
Important Bases	28
Acid–base Reactions	30

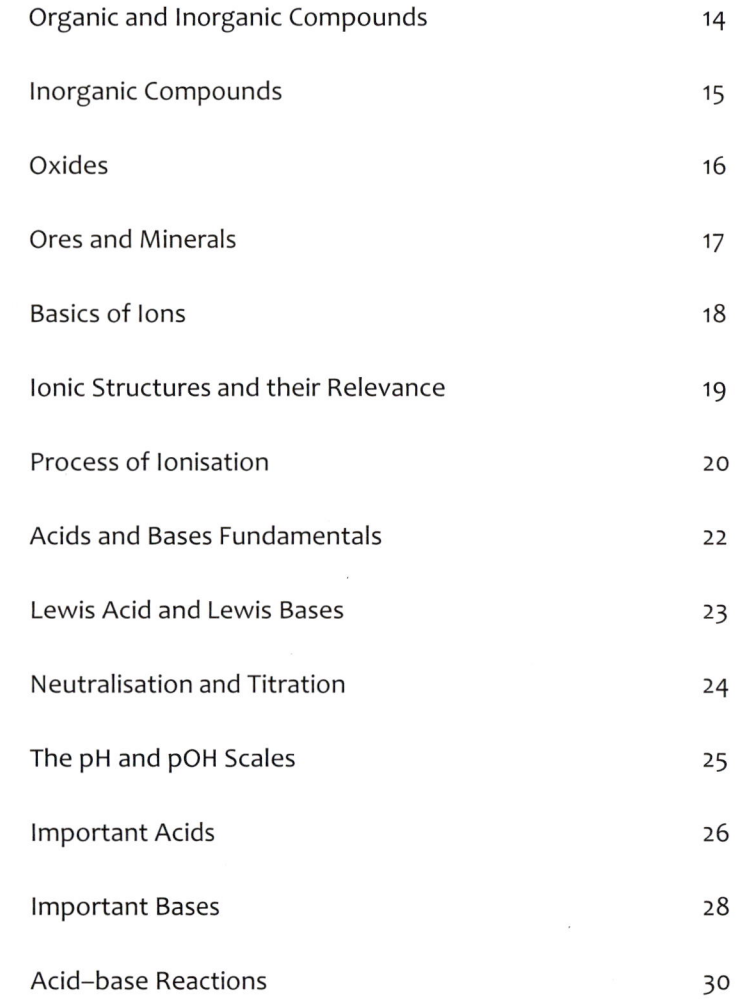

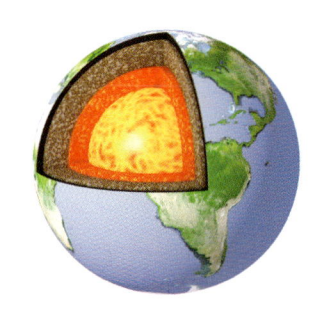

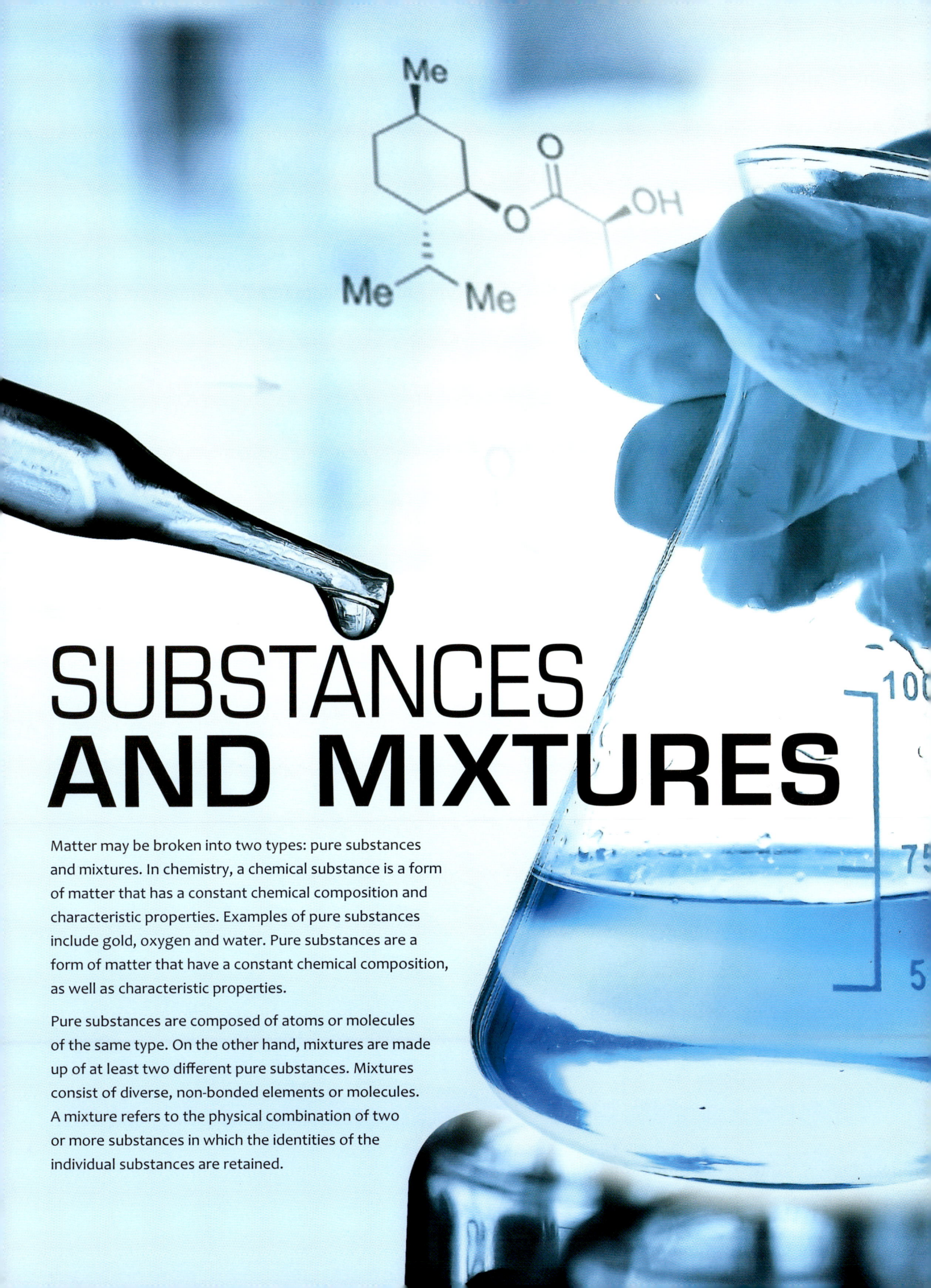

SUBSTANCES AND MIXTURES

Matter may be broken into two types: pure substances and mixtures. In chemistry, a chemical substance is a form of matter that has a constant chemical composition and characteristic properties. Examples of pure substances include gold, oxygen and water. Pure substances are a form of matter that have a constant chemical composition, as well as characteristic properties.

Pure substances are composed of atoms or molecules of the same type. On the other hand, mixtures are made up of at least two different pure substances. Mixtures consist of diverse, non-bonded elements or molecules. A mixture refers to the physical combination of two or more substances in which the identities of the individual substances are retained.

SCIENCE ENCYCLOPEDIA

What is a Substance?

A substance is a matter that bears a specific composition with specific properties. Any pure element can be a substance. Any pure compound can also be a substance. Chemical substances may be in the solid, liquid, gas or plasma state. Change in pressure or temperature may cause these substances to alter between different phases of matter.

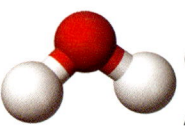

Chemical substance

A chemical substance is a type of matter that has a constant chemical composition and characteristic properties. In order to break a chemical substance into its components, one must separate its components or break its chemical bonds. Chemical substances can occur in solid, liquid, gas or plasma state. Substances can shift between the different phases of matter due to changes in temperature or pressure.

Pure chemical compound

A pure chemical compound is a chemical substance that comprises a specific set of molecules or ions that are chemically bonded. When two or more elements are combined into one substance through a chemical reaction, such as water, a chemical compound is formed. All compounds are substances, but not all substances are compounds. A chemical compound could either be various atoms bonded together in molecules, or crystals in which atoms, molecules or ions form a crystalline lattice. Compounds made mainly of carbon and hydrogen atoms are called organic compounds while all others are called inorganic compounds.

Why are some substances called "pure"?

Chemical substances are often called "pure" to distinguish them from mixtures. Pure water is an example of a chemical substance. It has the same properties and ratio of hydrogen to oxygen whether it is isolated from a river or made in a laboratory. Other chemical substances commonly witnessed in their pure form are diamond (carbon), gold, table salt (sodium chloride) and refined sugar (sucrose).

Steam and liquid water are two different forms of the same chemical substance, water.

Gold is a pure substance.

SUBSTANCES, MIXTURES AND COMPOUNDS

What is a Mixture?

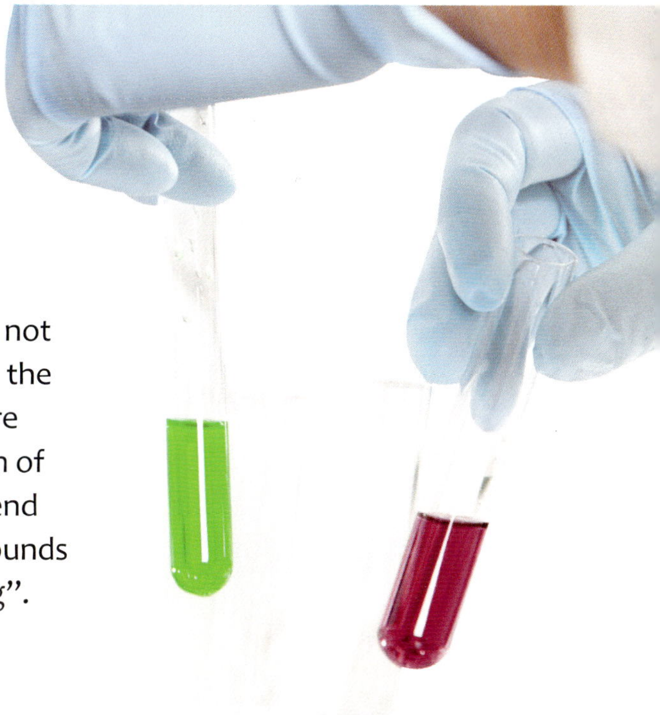

When two or more substances are mixed together but not chemically combined, the result is called a mixture. It is the physical combination of two or more substances, where their identities are retained and can be seen in the form of either suspensions, solutions or colloids. They are the end product of mixing chemical substances, such as compounds and elements by a process called "mechanical blending".

Azeotropes

Some mixtures may be separated into their components by applying physical, thermal and mechanical means. Azeotrope is the mixture that usually poses certain difficulties regarding the separation process required for obtaining their constituent (physical or chemical process or a blend).

Distillation and chromatography

On heating a liquid mixture, the liquid with the lowest boiling point is transformed into vapour and the other liquid is left behind. This process is called distillation and is used to separate alcohol from water.

Paper chromatography is used to isolate coloured mixtures, such as dyes or inks. In this method, coloured mixtures, travel at various speeds along the paper when a solvent is applied to them, thereby separating them from each other.

Separating mixtures

Several methods have been devised to separate mixtures. A common experiment performed in schools to test this approach is that of magnet and sand. The magnet attracts the iron filings to it, thus separating the iron filings from sand. Another separation method is called "centrifuging", which is used to separate particles or liquids from other liquids. This method uses the different densities of the substances that are present in the mixture as a means to separate the particles. The liquids in the mixture are separated into layers based upon their densities. This process uses a machine called a "centrifuge", which spins the test tubes containing the liquids at great speed.

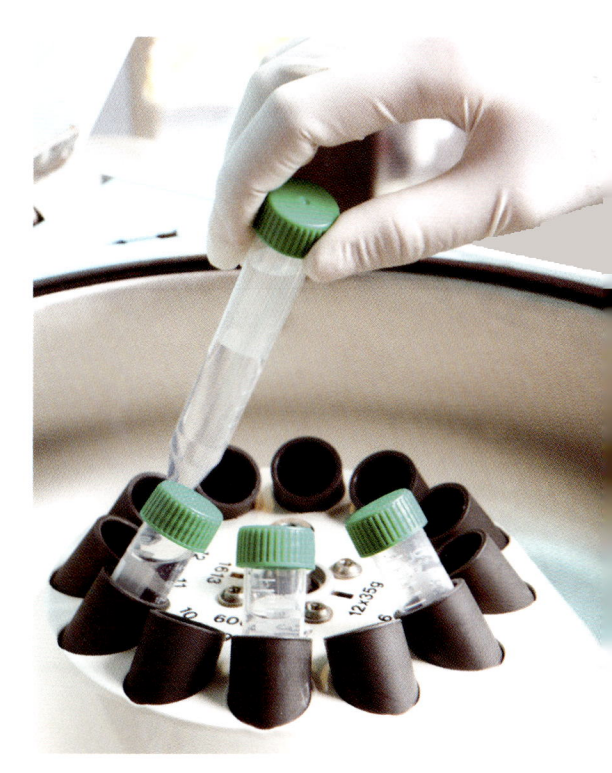

Samples in a centrifuge.

5

Types of Mixtures

A mixture is a substance in which two or more elements mix but don't chemically combine. Mixtures are usually classified into two broad groups: homogeneous or heterogeneous.

Homogeneous mixtures

When the components of a mixture are uniformly distributed, it is called a homogenous mixture. The chemical compositions of such mixtures are the same throughout. A single phase or state of matter is observed in a homogeneous mixture. Air, sugar, water, vinegar, detergent and steel are some examples of homogenous mixtures.

In a homogenous mixture, two or more components cannot be easily distinguished by sight. The composition of such mixtures is constant. It is more challenging to separate the components of a homogeneous mixture than to separate the components of a heterogeneous mixture.

Homogeneous mixture of a detergent.

Heterogeneous mixtures

A heterogeneous mixture is a mixture of two or more chemical substances, where different components of the mixture can be distinguished easily. These components can then be separated without much effort. Mixtures of sand and water or of sand and iron filings are examples of heterogeneous mixtures.

Heterogeneous mixture of water, oil and sand.

Heterogeneous vs homogeneous

Homogeneous and heterogeneous mixtures can be distinguished based on the scale of the sample. Any mixture is said to be heterogeneous on a small sampling scale because a sample could be as small as a single molecule. Practically speaking, if the property of interest is the same, irrespective of how much of the mixture is taken, then the mixture is a homogeneous one. We cannot pick out the components of a homogeneous mixture or use simple mechanical means to separate them. We cannot see or physically separate the components of a homogenous mixture, nor do they exist in various states of matter. On the other hand, in a heterogeneous mixture, the components of a mixture are not at all uniform, nor do they possess localised regions and distinctive properties like homogenous mixtures.

The terms "heterogeneous" and "homogeneous" are used to refer to the mixtures of materials. The difference among the two is the degree at which these materials have been mixed together along with the uniformity of their composition. Various samples from a mixture are not identical to each other. There are two or more phases in any heterogeneous mixture in which you can recognise a particular region with the properties that are different from those of a different region, even if they are the same form of matter (an example of this is a liquid or a solid). Examples of heterogeneous mixtures are vegetable soup, blood, the ice in soda, mixed nuts and soil.

SUBSTANCES, MIXTURES AND COMPOUNDS

Suspension mixture

A suspension mixture is created by mixing together two or more ingredients where the particles are large enough to be seen by the naked eye or with the use of a simple magnifying glass. The ingredients of a suspension mixture are heterogeneous. In fact, most heterogeneous mixtures are suspension mixtures.

- Solid–solid mix

These suspension mixtures consist of solids mixed with other solids. Bread mix is an example of visible solid particles that are stirred and mixed together. Soil is another example of a solid–solid suspension mixture as it contains dead organic matter, rocks, stones and pebbles. These mixtures can be separated by the simple process of sifting.

- Solid–liquid mix

If solid particles are mixed with a liquid to form a suspension mixture, the ingredients will separate with the heavier solid particles settling at the bottom. For example, if you mix sand and water, the sand would eventually sink to the bottom of the container. In case the solid particles are lighter than the liquid (as seen in the mixture of sawdust and water), they will separate and float to the top.

These mixtures can be separated by the processes of settling and filtration.

- Liquid–liquid mix

If drops of a liquid are mixed with another liquid or a gas solvent, the components can be separated. Once separated, if the droplets are heavier, they will settle at the bottom. If the droplets are lighter, they will float to the top.

- Size of particles

The size of solute particles in a colloidal mixture is much smaller than the particles in a suspension mixture. However, these particles are not as small as the particles in a solution. The particles in a colloidal mixture are typically as small as a clump of molecules that may not be visible even with a common microscope. What makes this kind of mixture rare is that the solute particles do not break down any further into single molecules. Thus, they form a solution.

- Blending

The blending of materials in a colloidal mixture is more forceful than the basic stirring done in a suspension mixture. Often, the materials of a colloidal mixture are violently mixed together. A good example is the concrete mixer machine that actively shakes the materials to minimise the particles settling to the bottom. Some examples of colloidal mixtures are mayonnaise, jello, fog, butter and whipped cream.

Solution

A solution is a homogeneous mixture, where one substance is dissolved in another substance. The solute dissolves in the solvent. Solutes may be solids, liquids or gases. The solvent is usually a liquid or a gas.

SCIENCE ENCYCLOPEDIA

Solubility

In simple words, "solubility" is the ability of a substance to dissolve in water or another liquid. A more precise definition would be that solubility is the maximum amount of solute that can be completely dissolved in a solvent under a given set of conditions.

Principal of solubility

On adding sugar or salt to a glass of water, the sugar or salt dissolves. If we continue to add more sugar or salt to that glass, there will come a point where no more sugar or salt can dissolve in it. This means that when an equilibrium is established between the solute (the component that dissolves in a solvent) and the solvent (able to dissolve a substance), then no more solute can dissolve in it. A solution that reaches this stage is called a "saturated solution". The excess of solute added to the solvent gets collected at the bottom of the solution.

Addition of salt in water.

Saturated solution

A solution that becomes saturated is said to have reached its limit or its "saturation point". Any more solute put into the solvent will not dissolve under normal conditions. There are many factors that can increase the limit of solubility such as temperature, pressure, the nature of its intermolecular forces or interionic forces of the solute and the solvent. When the solubility of a solute is increased, the solution is called a "supersaturated solution". Solubility gives us an insight into the properties of the substance we are dealing with. It also tells us the polarity that distinguishes the substance from other substances in a mixture and enables us to understand its applications.

Potassium permanganate dissolved in water.

FUN FACT

If you have a saturated solution of sugar, heating it will enable you to dissolve more sugar in it.

Solubility of barium sulphate.

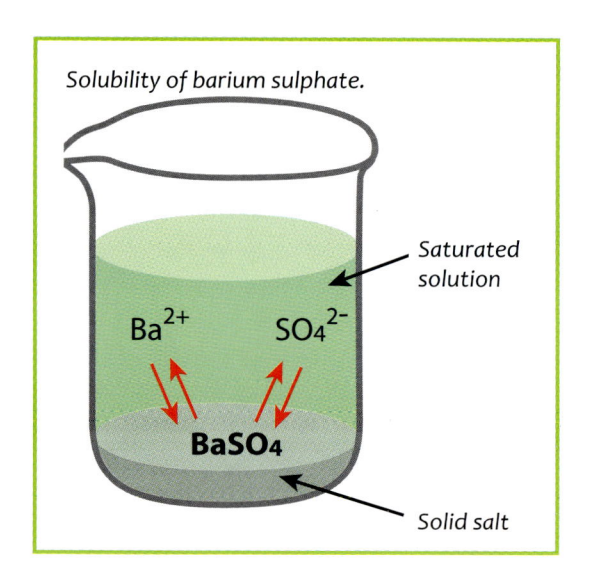

Saturated solution

Ba^{2+} SO_4^{2-}

BaSO₄

Solid salt

SUBSTANCES, MIXTURES AND COMPOUNDS

Solid Solution

A solid solution, as the name suggests, exists in the solid state. It is a solution composed of single or multiple solutes in one solvent. This variety of a mixture is regarded as a solution instead of a compound when the crystal construction of the solvent remains the same by inputting the solutes and when the mixture remains in a distinct homogeneous phase.

Coins made of copper (alloy).

Ability to mix

A solid solution can be distinguished from a manually made mixture of powdered solids, such as sugar and salt or salts. These manual mixtures have complete or limited ability to mix in the solid state. Instances of solid solutions mostly include moist solids, alloys and the crystallised salts in their liquid mixture.

Solid solution strengthening

With respect to alloys, intermetallic compounds (substances composed of definite proportions of two or more elemental metals) are frequently formed. The solute may include the solvent crystal lattice, by substituting a solvent particle in the lattice by adjusting itself into the gap between the solvent particles. Both these varieties of solid solutions influence the characteristics of the substance by altering the crystal lattice and interrupting the electric and physical homogeneousness of the solvent material. Solid solutions, according to the Hume-Rothery laws, are formed only if the solute and solvent have analogous atomic radii (15 per cent or less apart), identical crystal structure, similar electro-negativities and comparable valences. Thus, solid solutions are a blend of two crystalline solids that co-exist as a crystal lattice or a new variety of crystalline solid. Quite frequently, metal is strengthened by solid solution alloying and the mechanism is known as solid solution strengthening.

Strengthened metals have multiple uses.

SCIENCE ENCYCLOPEDIA

Key Properties of Substances

Substances are used for many types of applications, specifically because of their unique properties. Substance selection criteria entirely depends on the required key properties of a specific application. Some of the properties of substances are described as follows:

Conductivity

It is the fundamental property of matter that determines the ability of a substance to conduct an electric current through it. Its International System of Unit (SI unit) is Siemens per metre (S/m).

Density

It is the mass per unit volume of a substance. Mathematically, it is expressed as a ratio of mass and volume. Its physical system of unit or SI unit is kg/m^3. Density is the key property that we need to check for structural applications where lighter materials with more strength are preferred. Materials with higher density also find applications in various fields including military applications.

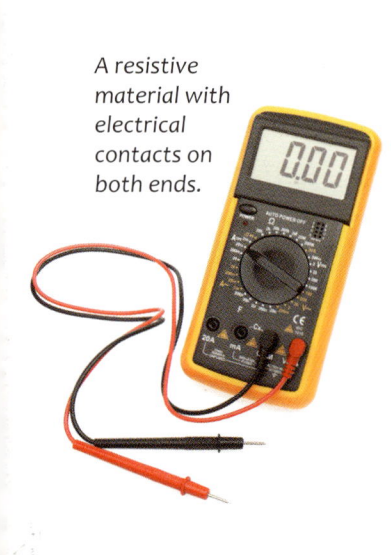

Copper wires can conduct electric currents.

A resistive material with electrical contacts on both ends.

Resistance

It is the basic property of matter that determines how strongly a substance opposes the flow of current through it. It is the reciprocal of conductivity. Its SI unit is ohm-metre (Ωm).

Ductility

The ductility of a substance is its ability to be stretched into a wire under tensile stress. It is a very important property to construct desired shapes.

Elasticity

It is the tendency of a solid matter to return to its original shape after being deformed by external forces. Mathematically, it is defined as the ratio of stress and strain.

Toughness

Toughness is the ability of a substance to absorb energy and transform without fracturing itself. Mathematically, it can be defined as the amount of energy per unit volume that a material can absorb before it is fractured. Its SI unit is Joule per cubic metre (J/m^3).

Malleability

It is the ability of a substance to be hammered into sheets under compressive stress. This property is found only in solids.

Gold sheets can be produced owing to gold's malleability.

10

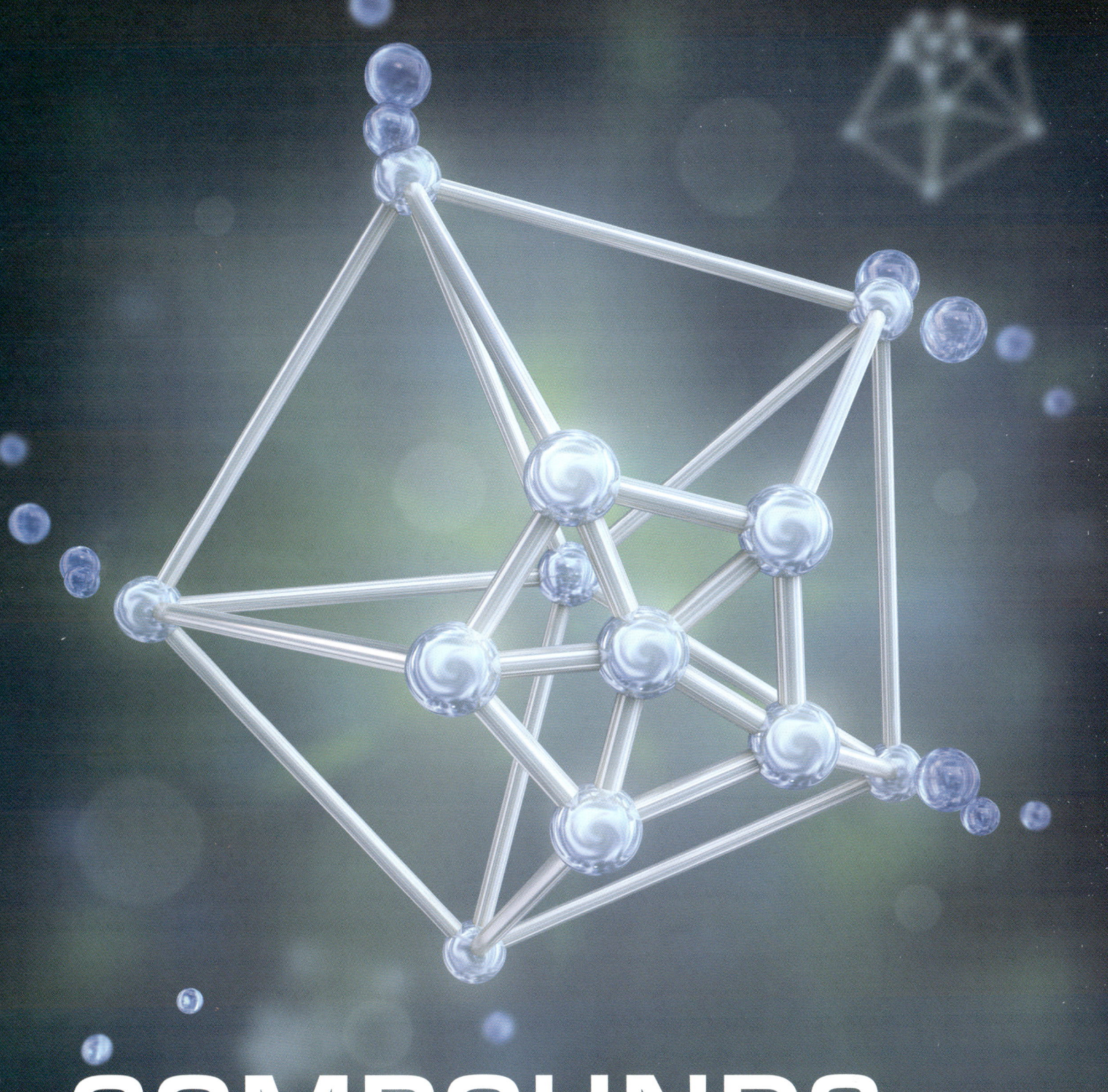

COMPOUNDS

In chemistry, a compound is a substance that is formed from the combination of two or more different elements in a way where the atoms are held together by chemical bonds that are tough to break. The resulting bond yields because of the sharing or exchange of electrons among the atoms.

The smallest, unbreakable unit of a compound is called a "molecule". The two types of chemical bonds that are common in compounds are the covalent bonds and the ionic bonds. The elements in any compound are always present in fixed ratios. Compounds can be decomposed chemically into their constituent elements.

SCIENCE ENCYCLOPEDIA

What is a Compound?

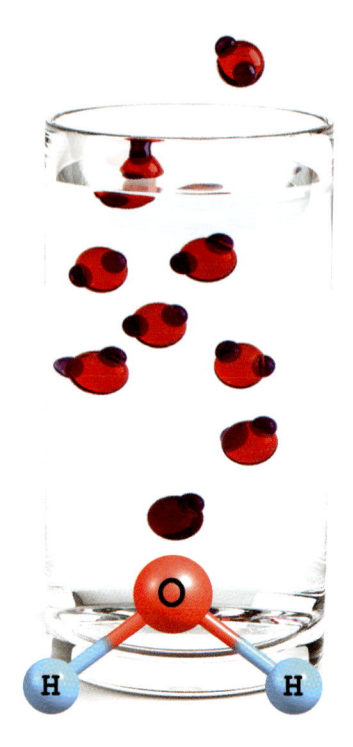

A compound can be defined as a substance that is formed by the atoms of two or more elements reacting chemically. Iron, copper, gold, carbon and hydrogen are all elements found in nature. But water is not an element. It is composed of two atoms of hydrogen and one atom of oxygen. These types of substances are called "compounds".

Characteristics of compounds

The characteristics of chemical compounds are different from the constituent elements from which they are formed. Some characteristics of compounds are as follows:

- The elements are present in a definite proportion in a compound and this proportion cannot be changed.
- A compound can be broken up into its constituent elements by various chemical reactions. But they cannot be broken up physically or mechanically.
- Compounds possess a definite and fixed chemical structure.
- Many types of bonds are found between the elements in a compound. These are covalent bonds, ionic bonds, coordinate bonds and metallic bonds.
- Most compounds are formed naturally as the elements are combined as a result of gaining stability.

Compounds have a specific chemical formula

Compounds are designated with a specific chemical formula. The hydrogen element is shown by the formula H_2 and oxygen by O_2. Water, a compound formed by hydrogen and oxygen, is shown by the formula H_2O. Compounds differ greatly from mixtures. The properties of a compound are completely different from its constituent elements. A mixture has the properties of its constituents. The constituents of a mixture can be separated by simple physical methods, whereas we cannot separate the constituents of a compound. Compounds are widely used in our daily life. They range from drinking water, salt, baking powder, bleaching powder and sugar to the gasoline that we use as fuel; the list is endless.

Types of compounds.

FUN FACT

We know that the chemical formula of water is H_2O. However, how many of us know its chemical name? The chemical name of water is dihydrogen monoxide denoting two atoms of hydrogen and one atom of oxygen in a molecule of water.

SUBSTANCES, MIXTURES AND COMPOUNDS

Classification and Structure of Compounds

Chemical compounds encompass a wide spectrum of substances; there are multiple ways of organising and classifying them. A primary way is by finding which compounds are formed by living organisms and which are not. The compounds that are synthesised as a product of the activity of living organisms are called organic compounds and those that are not, are called inorganic compounds. This classification has a number of notable exceptions, hence, they are now defined as compounds with significant carbon–carbon bonds.

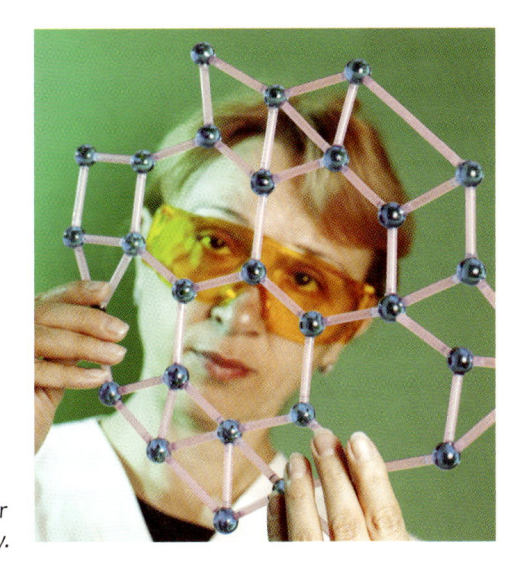

Scientist studying molecular geometry.

Chemical structure

The chemical structure of compounds can be analysed on three levels: molecular geometry (the structure of the microscopic molecules that constitute the compound), electronic structure (the configuration and the state of motion of the electrons forming the chemical bonds) and crystal structure (the comparatively large-scale systematic arrangement of the groups of molecules that recreate the entire macroscopic structure of the compound on repetition). On the microscopic level, it is often best approximated by its molecular geometry, which can be of many types, depending on the atoms forming the molecule, that is, their respective sizes, electronegativity, atomic number, etc.

Carbon dioxide (CO_2) is a naturally occurring chemical compound composed of oxygen atoms.

VSEPR

As per the quantum mechanical theory called the VSEPR, the bond length and the bond angle parameters can be used to classify molecular geometry into approximately 18 groups, such as linear, trigonal planar (carbon dioxide), trigonal pyramidal (boron trifluoride), octahedral (sulphur hexafluoride), etc.

SCIENCE ENCYCLOPEDIA

Organic and Inorganic Compounds

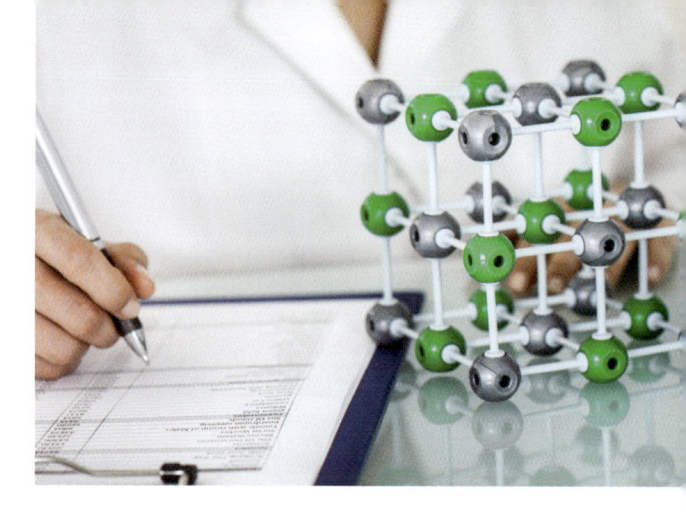

The field of chemistry that analyses organic compounds is called organic chemistry. The question that arises is – what are organic compounds? Compounds can be classified into organic and inorganic compounds. Organic compounds possess at least one carbon atom covalently bonded to another atom, preferably hydrogen, oxygen or nitrogen. All the compounds in which the C–H bond is found are called organic compounds, while the others are called inorganic compounds.

The definition

There is no accurate definition for organic compounds. Initially, it was believed that all compounds containing carbon atoms are called organic compounds; but there were many exceptions, like metal carbonyl, carbonates and cyanides, that were considered to be inorganic compounds. Subsequently, the "C–H" definition was found to be correct to a major extent. Organic compounds can be classified on the basis of the presence of the hitherto atoms or on their occurrence, namely, natural or synthetic. These compounds can also be classified into aliphatic and aromatic compounds. Aliphatic compounds are those possessing an open chain (C–H) structure and aromatic compounds are those possessing a carbon ring.

Methane is one of the simplest organic compounds. This image shows a methane burner with a flame used for cooking.

FUN FACT

Organic chemistry can be understood by studying carbon in nature as it is present in all the living beings present on Earth. Carbon is a non-metal.

Diamond is an inorganic compound.

The difference between organic and inorganic compounds

The presence of carbon atoms in organic compounds is the basic difference between organic and inorganic compounds. Organic compounds are mainly associated with living organisms. These primarily include nucleic acids, carbohydrates, fats, proteins, enzymes, DNA and methane. Inorganic compounds primarily include salt, diamond, carbon dioxide and metallic substances.

SUBSTANCES, MIXTURES AND COMPOUNDS

Inorganic Compounds

Inorganic chemistry is the study of elements and their properties from the periodic table, as well as the reactions and compounds formed among them. Fundamentally, all compounds that lack the presence of carbon atoms are called inorganic compounds. Berzelius depicted inorganic compounds as those that are not biological in origin and are inanimate.

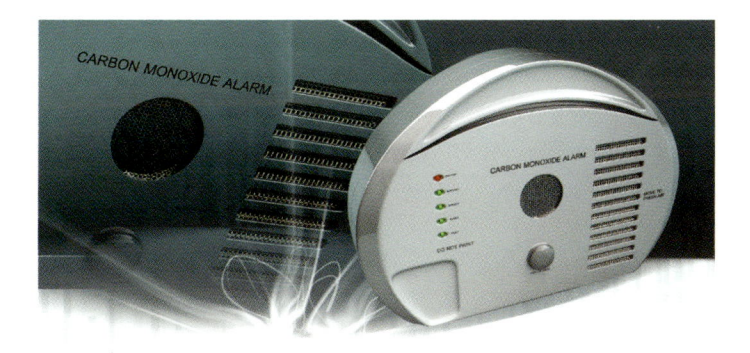

A fire alarm that detects carbon monoxide.

Nitrous oxide is also used in surgery and during pregnancy.

Some of them are listed below:

- Compounds like sodium, chloride, phosphate ions, carbonic acids, nitrogen, water, oxygen, carbon dioxide, etc., are essential for life.

- Coordination compounds have a wide variety of applications in various fields like photography, electroplating of silver, as oxidising agents, in estimating the hardness of water, in extraction, as dyeing agents, etc.

- Hard compounds like aluminium, copper, steel and bronze are used for making kitchen utensils.

- Oxides are also very useful. Nitrous oxide is also known as laughing gas. Water is a universal solvent.

- Many halides are used in greenhouse lamps and street lights. Sodium chloride is used in the common salt that we eat. Potassium chloride is used during cardiac surgery and in medicines.

- Carbonates are used in carbonated beverages, soaps, detergents, etc. They are also used in surgeries.

- The fields of applications of inorganic compounds are not limited and range from mining to medicine, from agriculture to fuel industries.

Metal halide lamp.

SCIENCE ENCYCLOPEDIA

Oxides

Oxides are a commonly found and important class of chemical compounds on Earth. They are made of molecules that have at least one oxygen atom and one other element, if not more. Oxygen is a highly electronegative element, which means that it has a high affinity to bond with other substances. The process by which an element or compound reacts with oxygen to form an oxide is called oxidation.

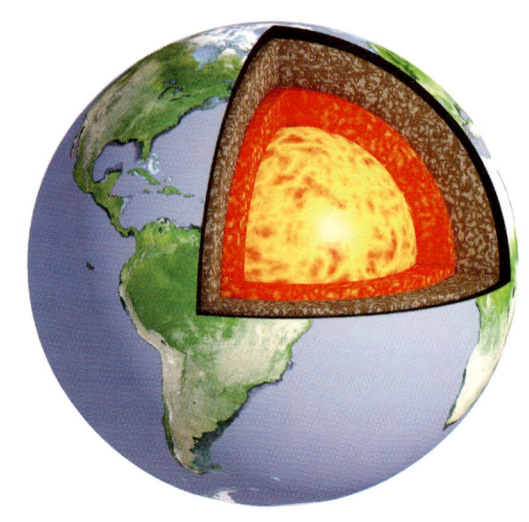

Oxides have many uses, from fire-proofing to vulcanising of rubber to being used as a colour pigment.

Uses of oxides

Some of the compounds that we encounter most commonly in our daily life are oxides. For example, the principal waste product of human respiration and an important constituent of plant nutrition is an oxide – carbon dioxide (CO_2). The reddish rust that develops on iron poles when exposed to open air for long periods is a hydrated oxide – ferric oxide (Fe_2O_3). Other important oxides are water (H_2O), without which life on Earth would have been impossible, calcium oxide (CaO), which is used to make mortar and concrete that holds buildings together, and nitrous oxide (N_2O), which is used as an anaesthetic during medical operations and for many other purposes.

Rusty oil lantern.

Oxidation of metals and non-metals

It is possible for metals and non-metals to attain their highest oxidation states (donate their maximum number of available valence electrons) in compounds with oxygen. Ionic oxides (compounds that contain the O_2) anion is formed by alkali metals and alkaline earth metals, as well as the transition metals and post-transition metals (in their lower oxidation states).

Oxidised metal showpiece.

Transformation from ionic to covalent bonds

Metals with high oxidation states form oxides whose bonds have a more covalent nature. Non-metals also form covalent oxides that are usually molecular in character. As you navigate the periodic table from the metals on the left to the non-metals on the right, a variation from ionic to covalent bonds in oxides is observed. A similar variation is observed in the reaction of oxides with water and the resulting acid-base character of the products. When ionic metal oxides react with water they produce hydroxides (compounds that contain an OH– ion). Most non-metal oxides react with water to produce acids.

SUBSTANCES, MIXTURES AND COMPOUNDS

Ores and Minerals

Chemical compounds are not found in their pure state in nature due to a large number of adulterating influences present in the natural environment. Instead, they are found in other crystalline naturally occurring inorganic compounds called minerals. These minerals are generally formed by large-scale geological processes rather than through the actions of living organisms.

All about the ore

Ores are a special category of minerals; they usually have a high percentage of a certain element, usually a metal, as one of their constituents. As such, it is often economically viable to isolate pure elements from particular ores rather than just any mineral that contains the element. For example, while aluminium is present in both clay as well as bauxite, only bauxite is used as an ore of aluminium because it is feasible to extract aluminium from it easily, cheaply and in large quantities. Therefore, every ore is a mineral, but every mineral is not an ore. Some very important ores are galena (PbS) for lead, acanthite (Ag_2S) for silver and magnetite (Fe_3O_4) for iron. The process of extracting pure elements from ores is called mining.

Difference between ores and minerals

- Ore comprises minerals; thus all the ores are minerals, but not all the minerals are ores.
- Ores are mineral deposits, whereas a mineral is a natural form in which the metals exist.
- Ores are used to extract metals economically. Therefore, in ores, a significant amount of metals are present.
- Ores can be defined as having an economical importance, whereas minerals are more scientifically important.

A crane digging at a mining site for ore.

SCIENCE ENCYCLOPEDIA

Basics of Ions

Atoms are the basic unit of an element. Electrons that revolve around the atoms in a circular path are sometimes lost or gained. This is when the atoms become positively or negatively charged and a positive or negative ion is formed. Thus, we can say that a charged atom, group of atoms or molecule is called an ion. It gets charged because the number of protons are not equal to the number of electrons.

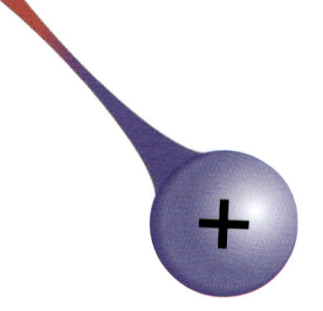

Types of ions

There are two types of ions:

- **Cation** – When an atom loses an electron, it gets positively charged. When this happens, a positively charged ion called cation is formed. For example, Na$^+$, Ca$^+$ and Fe$^+$.
- **Anion** – When an atom gains an electron, it gets negatively charged. When this happens, a negatively charged ion called anion is formed. For example, Cl$^-$ and P$^-$.

Types of Ions.

Classification of ions

Ions are classified depending on the number of atoms present, for example, monatomic, if one atom is present and polyatomic, if two or more atoms are present. English experimental physicist Michael Faraday introduced the term "ion" in 1834. If we look around, ions can be found everywhere, from thundering and lightning to salt dissolving in water. How we perceive the things that happen around us depends upon us.

Charge of an ion

In order to figure out what the charge of an ion should be, one must remember the following:

- The number of charges on an ion formed by a metal is equal to the group number of the metal.
- The number of charges on an ion formed by a non-metal is equal to the group number minus eight.

Ionic bonds

When metals react with non-metals, there is a transfer of electrons from metal atoms to the non-metal atoms, forming ions. As a result, an ionic compound is formed. Let us consider some reactions between metals and non-metals:

Sodium + chlorine = sodium chloride

Magnesium + oxygen = magnesium oxide

The metal atoms give electrons to the non-metal atoms in each of these reactions; the metal atoms become positive ions and the non-metal ones become negative ions. When a non-metal forms a bond, the ending name changes. In these reactions, the ending is "–ide", showing that only one element is present. If the ending was "–ate", it means that oxygen is also present in the molecule of the element.

FUN FACT

While mentioning an ionic compound, the positive ion is named first, followed by the negative ion. That is why table salt is written as (Na$^+$ and Cl$^-$) NaCl.

All batteries run on ionic reactions.

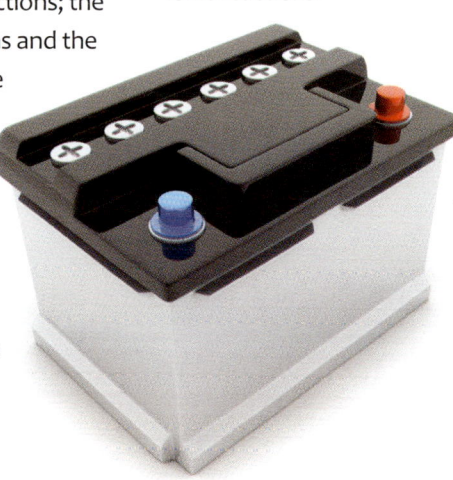

SUBSTANCES, MIXTURES AND COMPOUNDS

Ionic Structures and their Relevance

An atom consists of three types of particles: protons, neutrons and electrons. The negatively charged electrons, revolving around the atom in circular paths called orbits, can be very easily subtracted or added to an atom. When this addition or subtraction of electrons from an atom occurs, charged particles called ions are formed. The numerous arrangements of these ions form different ionic structures having different physical, chemical and electrical properties.

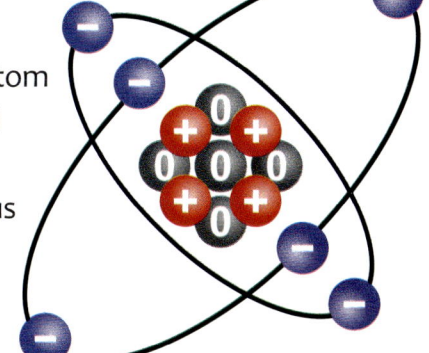

Example of ionic compounds

Magnesium oxide (MgO), calcium chloride (CaCl$_2$), sodium fluoride (NaF) and potassium oxide (K$_2$O) are a few examples of ionic compounds. These compounds are very easy to identify as they are metal and non-metal bonded compounds. When an atom loses its electrons, it becomes positively charged, forming a positively charged ion and when electrons are gained by an atom, a negatively charged ion is formed. The attraction between the positively and negatively charged ions form ionic compounds having different ionic structures. Different arrangements of ions are possible to create ionic structures.

Pink crystal salt.

Abstract geometric lattice with the scope of molecules.

Co-ordination number

The number of cations (negatively charged ions) around each anion (positively charged ions) is called its co-ordination number. In addition, the coordination number depends on the stoichiometry (the relationship between the substances forming a compound) and the size of the atoms; for example, Na$^+$Cl$^-$, in which Na$^+$ has a co-ordination number of six as there are six anions around a sodium cation. The bonding forces between the positive and negative ions in ionic structures result in different properties. Few properties of the ionic compounds are that they have high melting and boiling points due to the strong attraction between the ions. They have high enthalpies of fusion and vaporisation, again due to bonding forces. They are usually tough to break. Ionic solids like Na$^+$Cl$^-$ do not conduct electricity, though they can conduct it in an aqueous solution or molten form. They mostly exist in crystalline form, such as KCl.

Lattice

Metals form structures that are packed spheres. The different arrangements of atoms, ions or molecules in solid state substances are called lattice. Mostly, in ionic compounds, anions are larger than the cations. In such cases, we consider a close packed arrangement of anions. These arrangements are cubic close packing (ccp) and hexagonal close packing (hcp). The radius ratio determines the position of the cation in the ionic structures. A radius ratio is defined as the ratio of the radius of the cation to the radius of an ion.

SCIENCE ENCYCLOPEDIA

Process of Ionisation

The formation of ions by the loss and gain of electrons is called ionisation. The amount of energy required to remove the electrons from a neutral atom in the gaseous state is called ionisation energy. The unit of ionisation energy is not fixed. There can be many levels of ionisation energy; first level "i1", second level "i2" and so on.

Ionisation energy

The energy required to remove the second electron from an atom is more than removing the first electron. Electrons that have small orbits and are closer to the protons experience more force of attraction. Thus, they require more ionisation energy. Hence, it is concluded that as we move right in the periodic table, ionisation energy gradually increases. It decreases as we move from top to the bottom in the periodic table because the nuclear radius decreases and hence, more energy is required to remove the electrons. The process is very commonly used in numerous instruments in the research field, like mass spectrometer, and the medical field, like radiotherapy.

FUN FACT

Crystallisation occurs because of ionisation as well. When water is supersaturated with alum, a lot of ions are formed that float freely. In this saturated solution, if you were to suspend a thread, the alum ions would deposit on it, forming a string of crystals.

Electron capture ionisation

Anions are produced when free electrons collide with any atom and get trapped in the barrier caused by the electric potential, by releasing the excess energy. This process is commonly known as electron capture ionisation. Cations are formed by transferring the energy to the bound electron to release it. Threshold energy is required to knock out the electrons and is known as the ionisation potential.

An ionic chamber.

Ion formation.

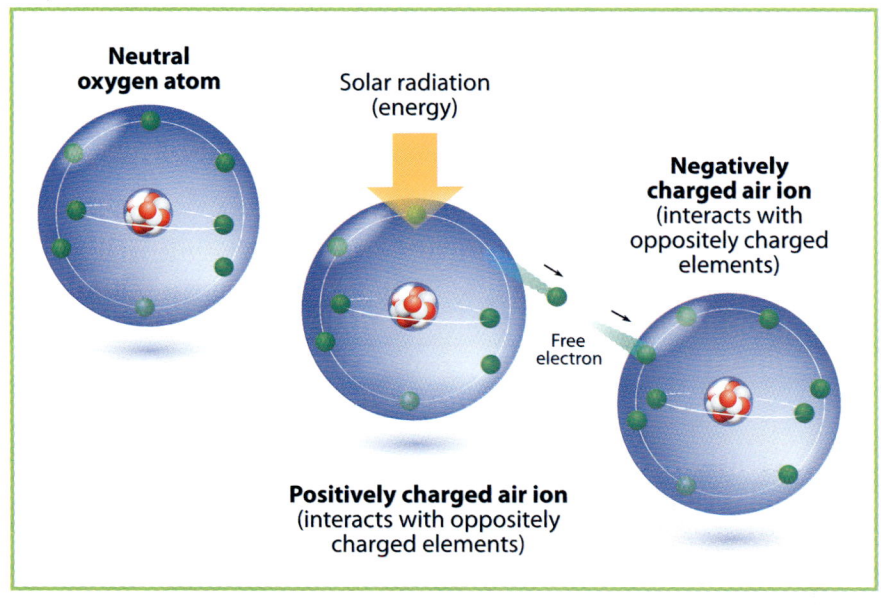

Neutral oxygen atom

Solar radiation (energy)

Positively charged air ion (interacts with oppositely charged elements)

Free electron

Negatively charged air ion (interacts with oppositely charged elements)

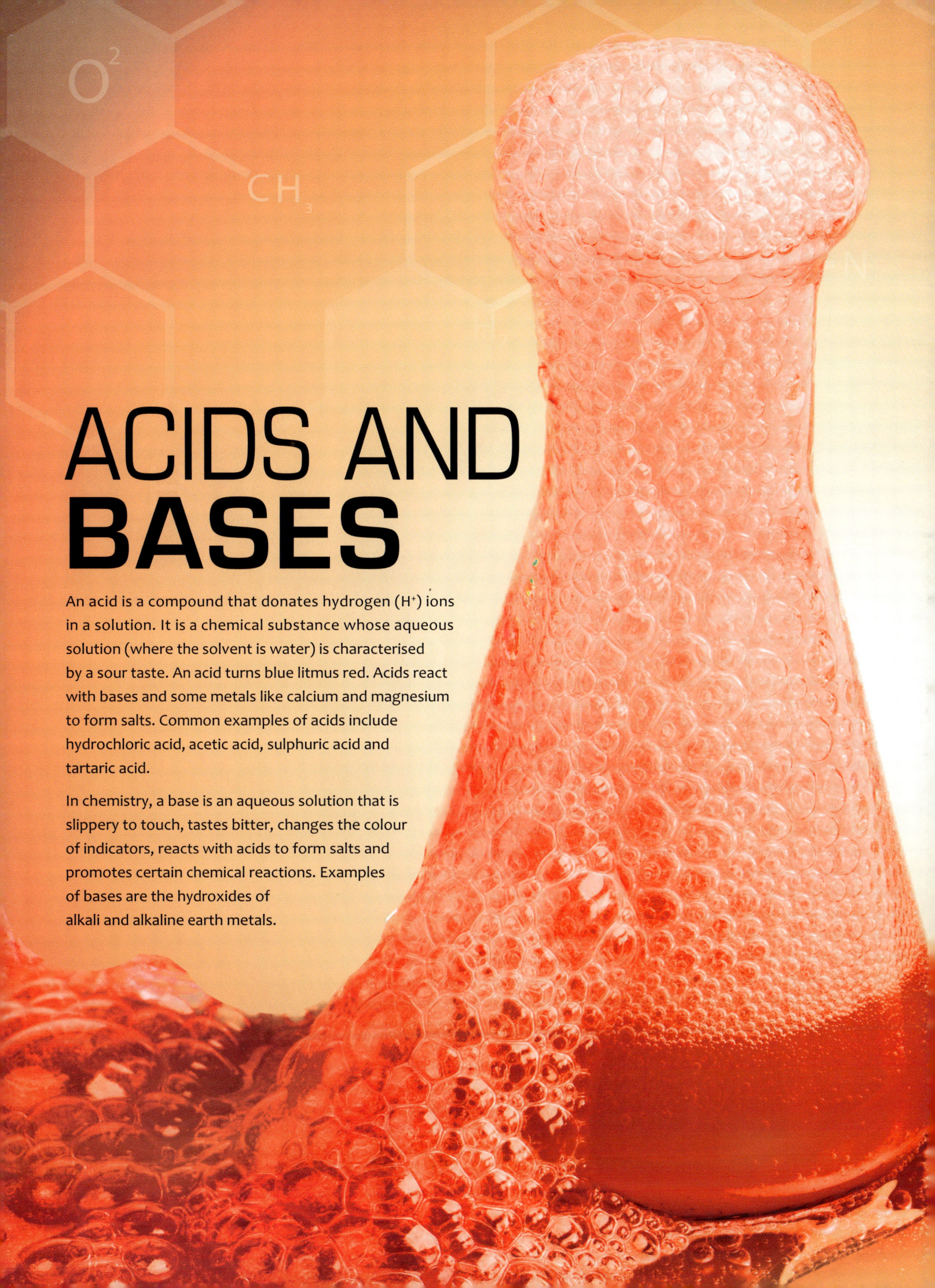

ACIDS AND BASES

An acid is a compound that donates hydrogen (H⁺) ions in a solution. It is a chemical substance whose aqueous solution (where the solvent is water) is characterised by a sour taste. An acid turns blue litmus red. Acids react with bases and some metals like calcium and magnesium to form salts. Common examples of acids include hydrochloric acid, acetic acid, sulphuric acid and tartaric acid.

In chemistry, a base is an aqueous solution that is slippery to touch, tastes bitter, changes the colour of indicators, reacts with acids to form salts and promotes certain chemical reactions. Examples of bases are the hydroxides of alkali and alkaline earth metals.

SCIENCE ENCYCLOPEDIA

Acids and Bases Fundamentals

The term acid is derived from the Latin term *acidus*, which means sour. Swedish scientist Svante Arrhenius defined an acid as "a chemical substance which, when dissolved in water, gives an hydrogen (H$^+$) ion and combines with the water molecule to form the hydronium ion (H$_3$O$^+$)". Acids are also characterised by their ability to react with bases and neutralise them.

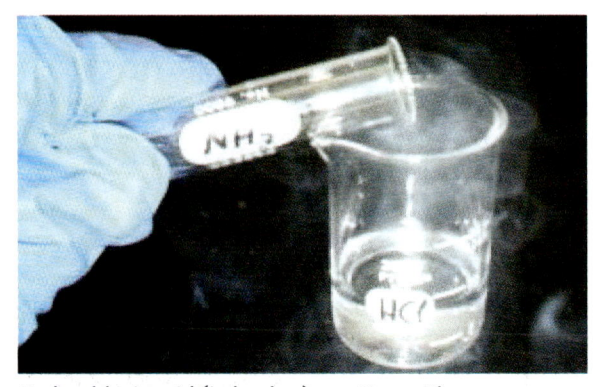

Hydrochloric acid (in beaker) reacting with ammonia fumes to produce ammonium chloride (white smoke).

Determining an acid

Any chemical substance whose aqueous solution tastes sour is either an acid or contains a certain amount of acid. However, the standard test for acidity is conducted using the litmus test, during which an acid can turn blue litmus paper red. An acid can also be defined as a substance that donates H$^+$ ions and when an acid is dissolved in water, the balance between the H$^+$ ions and hydroxide (OH$^-$) ions shifts. As, an acid donates H$^+$ ions, water has more H$^+$ ions than OH$^-$ ions and the solution is called acidic. The pH value (scale used to measure acidity/alkalinity of a substance) of acids is less than seven. Examples of acids are sulphuric acid, nitric acid, hydrochloric acid and oxalic acid.

What is a base?

A base is a substance that can accept protons or H$^+$ ions. Its properties are opposite to that of an acid. It turns red litmus paper blue. Not all bases dissolve in water and those that do are known as alkalis. Bases usually taste bitter. According to Arrhenius, they give OH$^-$ ions in an aqueous solution. Bases react with acids and neutralise each other to form a salt and water. This is called an acid–base reaction.

Accepting ions

A base can also be defined as a substance that accepts H$^+$ ions. Thus, when an acid is dissolved in water, the balance between the H$^+$ ions and OH$^+$ ions shifts in the opposite direction. As bases soak H$^+$ ions, water has fewer H$^+$ ions than OH$^-$ ions and the solution is called alkaline. The pH value of alkaline solutions is greater than seven. Examples of bases are baking soda, milk of magnesia and ammonia solution.

pH indicators and tube with pH values.

SUBSTANCES, MIXTURES AND COMPOUNDS

Lewis Acid and Lewis Bases

Apart from Arrhenius, other scientists have also given definitions of acids and bases, as there are many other chemicals that exhibit certain acidic and basic properties even though they may strictly not give an H⁺ ion or OH⁻ radical.

Classification of Lewis acid and base

GN Lewis proposed a definition, which focussed on electron transfer rather than proton transfer. A Lewis acid reacts with a Lewis base to form a Lewis adduct. A Lewis acid is a chemical species that accepts an electron pair and a Lewis base is a chemical that donates an electron pair to form the adduct. Trimethylborane (Me_3B) is a Lewis acid and ammonia (NH_3) is a Lewis base. Their adduct is represented as $Me_3B:NH_3$. The ":" means that a chemical bond is formed between the two chemical compounds. The adduct has a bond that is something between a covalent and an ionic bond.

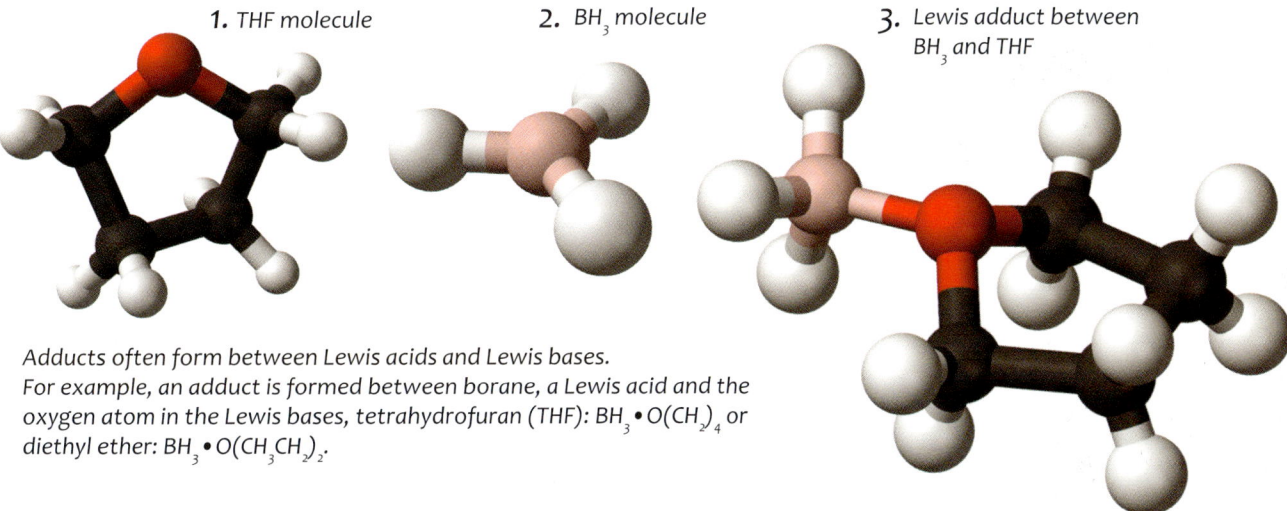

1. THF molecule

2. BH_3 molecule

3. Lewis adduct between BH_3 and THF

Adducts often form between Lewis acids and Lewis bases. For example, an adduct is formed between borane, a Lewis acid and the oxygen atom in the Lewis bases, tetrahydrofuran (THF): $BH_3 \bullet O(CH_2)_4$ or diethyl ether: $BH_3 \bullet O(CH_3CH_2)_2$.

Structure

Lewis acids usually have a triangular planar molecular structure. Examples are boron trifluoride (BF_3), aluminium chloride ($AlCl_3$) or even more complex compounds, such as $Et_3Al_2Cl_2$. As seen from this example, Lewis acids are also chemicals with metal cations.

The Lewis base has a highly occupied molecular orbital. These include amines of the formula NH_3-xRx (where R is an alkyl or aryl), phosphines of the formula PR_3-xAx (where R is an alkyl, A is an aryl) and compounds of S, Se, O and Te having oxidation state 2.

Boron trifluoride in 3D. It is a useful Lewis acid and a versatile building block for other boron compounds.

SCIENCE ENCYCLOPEDIA

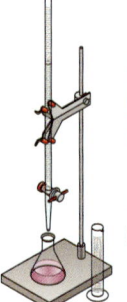

Neutralisation and Titration

A chemical reaction in which an acid and a base reacts quantitatively so that no excess acid or base is left is called a neutralisation reaction. After such a reaction reaches its equivalence point (when equal quantities of acid and base mix together), the number of H⁺ ions in the solution is equal to the number of OH⁻ ions in the solution. Therefore, nothing besides salt and water remains.

A salt is an ionic compound that results from the neutralisation reaction of an acid and a base.

Analysis of soil samples by titration.

Titration

Titration is the process of chemical analysis where the quantity of a constituent of a sample is determined by adding an exactly known quantity of another substance to the measured sample with which the desired constituent reacts in a definite and known proportion. This process is conducted by gradually adding a standard solution (a solution of known concentration) of a titrant using a burette. The addition of this standard solution is stopped when the equivalence point is reached.

How does it work?

A simple example would be:
$HCl + NaOH = NaCl + H_2O$

In this reaction, hydrochloric acid (HCl) and sodium hydroxide (NaOH) are taken in equal amounts, that is, the number of H⁺ ions that HCl will give rise to in the aqueous solution is equal to the number of OH⁻ ions that NaOH will give rise to in the solution.

Concentration of acid

Titration is employed to find out the equivalence point. Titration is a method in which we can analyse the concentration of an analyte (substance whose properties are being analysed) in a solution or, in this case, the concentration of an acid in water. Take a certain amount of acidic solution in a conical flask along with a small litmus paper or phenolphthalein. The solution will be red or pink in colour. Now, add a base from a burette drop by drop until the solution becomes colourless, that is, until it becomes neutral or reaches its equivalence point. After finding out how much of a basic solution with a known concentration and molarity (measure of concentration of a solution) is required to neutralise an acidic solution of known molarity but unknown concentration, we can find out the concentration of the acid.

SUBSTANCES, MIXTURES AND COMPOUNDS

The pH and pOH Scales

Acidity or alkalinity are measured using a logarithmic scale known as the pH scale. Soren Peder Lauritz Sorensen proposed the concept of pH in 1909. A strong acidic solution may have a million times more H⁺ ions than a strong basic solution. A strong basic solution may have a million times more OH⁻ ions than a strong acidic solution. To deal with such large numbers, scientists take the help of a logarithmic scale, known as the pH scale, which is basically pH = –log [H⁺], where [H⁺] is the concentration.

Chart showing the variation of colour of universal indicator paper with pH.

Standard scale for acids

The pH scale is a standardised scale that is used to measure the acidity or basicity of an aqueous solution. The scale ranges from 0 to 14. A solution with pH that is below seven is acidic, while a solution with pH that is above seven is basic. Therefore, the pH of a neutral solution should, by theory, be seven. Pure water has a pH that is very close to seven, but not exactly seven. It is important to note that the pH of an acid cannot be zero in practice.

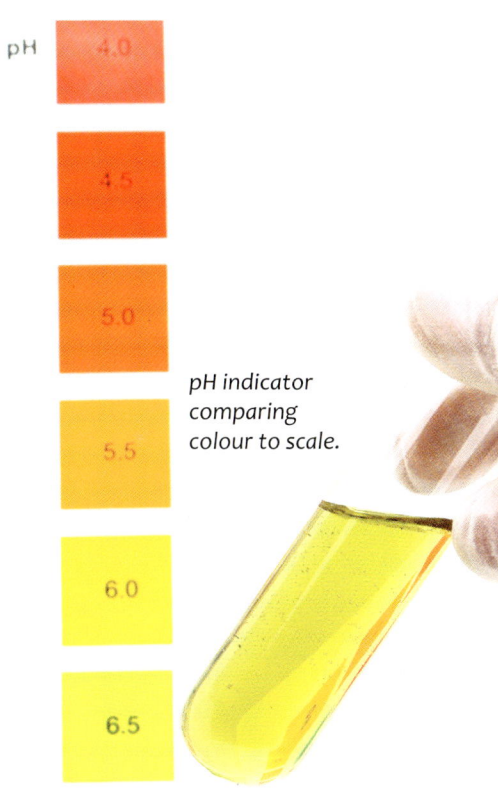

pH indicator comparing colour to scale.

Standard scale for bases

The pOH scale is similar to the pH scale. It measures the concentration of OH⁻ ions. It is a scale used to show the concentration of OH⁻ ions in a solution. This scale is based on the molarity of hydroxide ions in a solution with the formula pOH = –log [OH⁻].

Bases cannot have a pH of 14 or greater in practice. It is actually the negative logarithm of activity of the hydronium (H₃O⁺) ion. pOH is approximately equal to 14 – pH.

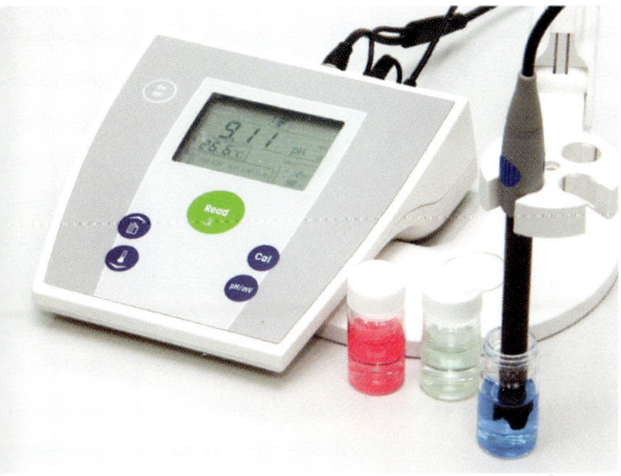

pH meter to measure the acidity-alkalinity of liquids.

Reading the pH scale

The pH of a solution is measured using a pH meter, which gives pH readings of the difference in electromotive force (voltage) between suitable electrodes placed in the solution to be tested. Basically, a pH meter constitutes a voltmeter attached to a pH-responsive electrode and a reference electrode.

SCIENCE ENCYCLOPEDIA

Important Acids

Acids that ionise (convert into ions by losing electrons) completely in a solution are called strong acids. An acid that leaves very little ionisation is a weak acid. Strong acids reduce the pH for a given molarity of a solution. Let us look at some common and important acids. Food items like lemon, raw mango, orange and curd taste sour as they contain acids.

Hydrochloric acid (HCl)

Hydrochloric acid is a strong acid. It ionises almost completely in water. It is colourless in appearance but has a very strong, irritating odour. It exists in the liquid form. It is formed by dissolving hydrogen chloride (a colourless gas) in water. As soon as the gas comes in contact with water, it sinks and mixes well with it.

FUN FACT

Dilute hydrochloric acid actually exists in our stomach and aids in the digestion of food. It has a pH between 1 and 2.

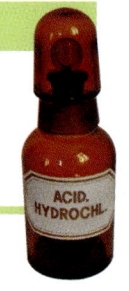

Hydrochloric acid is packaged and marketed in small containers for use in laboratories.

Citric acid ($H_3C_6H_5O_7$)

The most common sources of citric acid are fruits, such as tomatoes and lemons. Citric acid belongs to the carboxylic acid family. It is a colourless acid that forms a crystalline organic compound. It is present in almost all plants and even in the tissues and fluids of certain animals. It breaks down fats, carbohydrates and proteins into water and carbon dioxide. Citric acid was first removed from lemon juice by a chemist named Carl Wilhelm Scheele in 1784, using a fungus named *Aspergillus niger*. Citric acid aids in the production of sugar and molasses. It is also used to add flavour to various aerated drinks and sweets. It is also used in solutions that aid in the cleaning of metals, as well as to stabilise certain food items.

Lemons, oranges, limes and other citrus fruits possess high concentrations of citric acid.

Acetic acid ($HC_2H_3O_2$)

Acetic acid is a weak acid. It ionises very weakly with water. Acetic acid is also called ethanoic acid and it belongs to the carboxylic acid group. Vinegar is produced after a dilute solution of acetic acid is fermented and oxidised by natural carbohydrates. Acetate is a salt or ester of acetic acid. Metal acetates are prepared in industries in order to be used in printing presses.

Vinegar (produced from acetic acid) has a pH of 4.

SUBSTANCES, MIXTURES AND COMPOUNDS

Drops of concentrated sulphuric acid rapidly dehydrate a piece of cotton towel.

Sulphuric acid (H_2SO_4)

Sulphuric acid is a strong acid. It completely ionises in water. Sulphuric acid is used extensively in chemical industries. It is also known as hydrogen sulphate or "oil of vitriol". It is a colourless acid that has an oily texture. Like nitric acid, sulphuric acid is a corrosive liquid. It is an important acid, as well as an important chemical for industries and is prepared as a result of its reaction with water and sulphur trioxide.

Sulphuric acid is used to prepare pigments, various drugs, fertilisers, detergents, inorganic acids and salts, explosives and dyes. Sulphuric acid is used in petroleum refineries. It is also used to store batteries.

Nitric acid (HNO_3)

Nitric acid is a strong acid that almost completely ionises in water. It is a highly corrosive liquid and colourless in appearance. As an acid, it can burn the human skin upon contact and is highly toxic to human beings. In water, nitric acid decomposes into nitrogen dioxide and oxygen, thus forming a yellowish brown solution with water. It is used in industries as one of the ingredients for fertilisers and explosives. Nitric acid reacts with ammonia to form ammonium nitrate, which is used to make fertilisers. It mixes with glycerol and toluene to form explosives like nitroglycerin and trinitrotoluene. Nitric acid is also used in the preparation of dyes and plastics.

Fuming nitric acid contaminated with yellow nitrogen dioxide.

Carbonic acid (H_2CO_3)

Carbonic acid is a weak acid. It barely ionises in water. It is created by the reaction of carbon dioxide with water. When carbon dioxide dissolves in water, it forms carbonic acid. Carbonic acid sometimes appears in rain when carbon dioxide dissolves in rain water. When this carbonic acid gives up one hydrogen ion, it forms a bicarbonate ion. It is mainly used in aerated drinks and can be found in blood and champagne. Carbonic acid keeps the pH level of our body stable. Hence, people are advised to consume lemons and tomatoes.

The tiny bubbles on the surface are proof that carbonic acid is present in champagne.

SCIENCE ENCYCLOPEDIA

Important Bases

A strong base is a base that completely ionises in a solution. For example, sodium hydroxide is a strong base. On the other hand, a base that does not ionise completely or ionises very little in a solution is called a weak base. Sodium bicarbonate is a weak base. A strong base has a strong pH with the morality of a solution. Caustic soda and baking soda are slippery to the touch and have a bitter taste as they are bases.

Sodium bicarbonate (NaHCO3)

Sodium bicarbonate is a weak base. It is also called "baking soda". You might have seen it being used in cakes. It ionises very little in water. The reaction for baking soda or sodium bicarbonate is:

$NaHCO_3 + H_2O = H_2CO_3 + OH^- + Na^+$

Sodium bicarbonate comes in very fine and soft particles.

How do cakes "rise"?

When sodium bicarbonate comes in contact with an acid, the reaction gives out carbon dioxide. The reaction is indicated as:

$NaHCO_3 + H^+ = Na^+ + H_2O + CO_2$ (carbon dioxide)

The above reaction takes place while baking a cake or cupcake. This is because baking powder has portions of sodium bicarbonate and cream of tartar, which is a weak acid. These do not react with each other unless they have been mixed with water, which is added at the time of cooking or baking.

Cakes tend to rise because sodium bicarbonate releases carbon dioxide in the mixture.

Gluten and puff pastries

Have you heard of food items with gluten in them? Gluten is another ingredient that allows foam to form in the mixture. The mixture for biscuits is beaten vigorously and mixed with gluten in order to create a foam.

Puff pastes are used to create pastries. The pastry mixtures are expanded by the use of steam or water vapour.

Puff pastries are named so due to their "puffiness", which they get due to baking soda.

SUBSTANCES, MIXTURES AND COMPOUNDS

Sodium bicarbonate as a medicine

Sodium bicarbonate is not only used to cook and bake, but also used as a medicine for minor problems. Sodium bicarbonate is prescribed as a medicine for heartburn, acid indigestion and for the reduction of the acidic content in blood or urine. Sodium bicarbonate might come in the form of tablets or powders, which need to be taken orally. Usually, when used as an antacid, sodium bicarbonate needs to be taken at least within two hours after a meal. This medicine is also used to increase the amount of sodium in one's body.

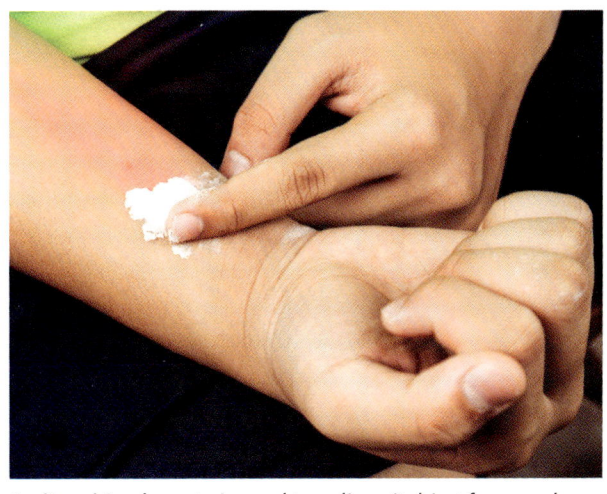

Sodium bicarbonate is used to relieve itching from rashes.

Sodium bicarbonate as a leavening agent

Many baked goods have a porous surface, which is created by the release of the gases present within. While these gases are released, the baked goods expand more than the original container and rise. The substance that causes all of this is called the "leavening agent".

During this process, the person producing the baked goods is required to continuously and vigorously mix the ingredients that need to expand or rise. This is in order to allow air bubbles and foam to be produced within the mixture. Egg whites are widely used in baked goods as they enable strong foams to form within the mixture.

Egg whites used in baked goods enable strong foams to form within the mixture.

Side-effects of sodium bicarbonate

Sodium bicarbonate, when taken in excess or small dosages, might cause gas and stomach cramps. Some might begin to feel more thirsty than usual. However, this is a minor side-effect.

Sodium hydroxide (NaOH)

Sodium hydroxide is considered to be a strong base. It is also called "caustic soda". Sodium hydroxide exists in solid state as an odourless crystalline substance. It tends to absorb the moisture present in the air. When this solid is dissolved in water, it releases heat, which is then used as a means to ignite flammable materials. Sodium hydroxide is corrosive in nature and is mainly used as a solid or as a solution with only 50 per cent of sodium hydroxide.

It is used in the manufacture of rayon, paper, dye and petroleum products. Sodium hydroxide is used to process cotton and other natural fabrics. It is also used to clean, bleach and launder other metal substances. Sodium hydroxide is used to clean commercial ovens and drains. Sodium hydroxide is corrosive to animal and plant tissue. However, it is used in most industries as an industrial alkali.

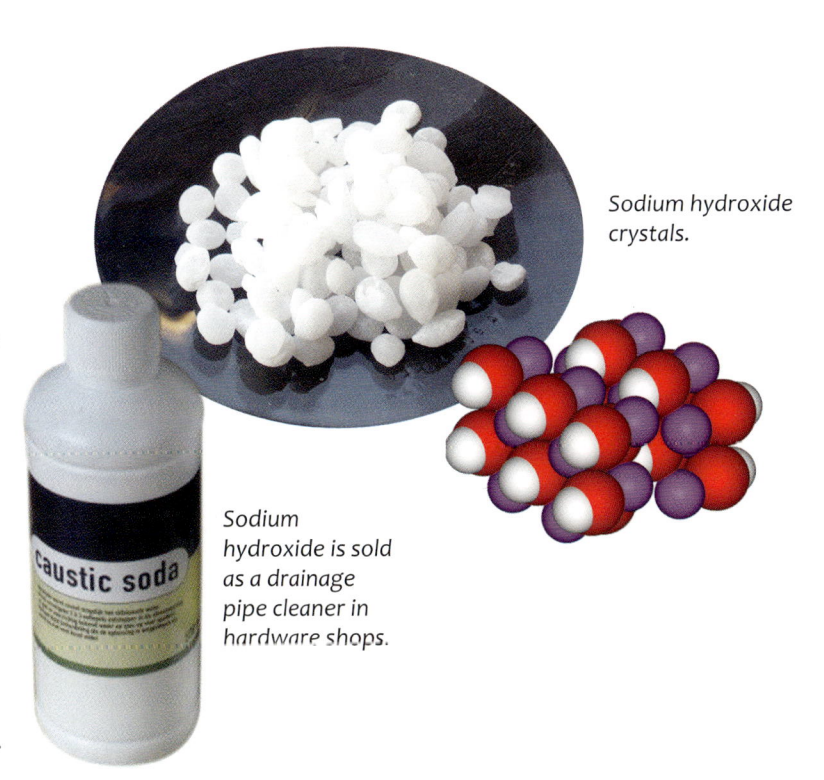

Sodium hydroxide crystals.

Sodium hydroxide is sold as a drainage pipe cleaner in hardware shops.

29

SCIENCE ENCYCLOPEDIA

Acid–base Reactions

An acid and base react with each other when they are brought together. Their reaction causes a neutralisation of properties to take place in both the acid and the base, so that a salt is formed. This reaction produces water as the H+ cation of the acid mixes with the OH– anion of the base. It forms a compound called "salt".

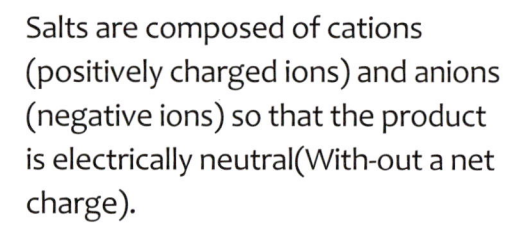

Salts are composed of cations (positively charged ions) and anions (negative ions) so that the product is electrically neutral(With-out a net charge).

Different acids and bases react with each other to form different salts.

Basic salt
A salt that is the product of the neutralization of a strong base and a weak acid.

Hydrolysis
A chemical process of decomposition involving the splitting of a bond and the addition of the hydrogen cation and the hydroxide anion of water.

Hydroxide
An univalent anion (OH-1) based on the hydroxyl functional group.

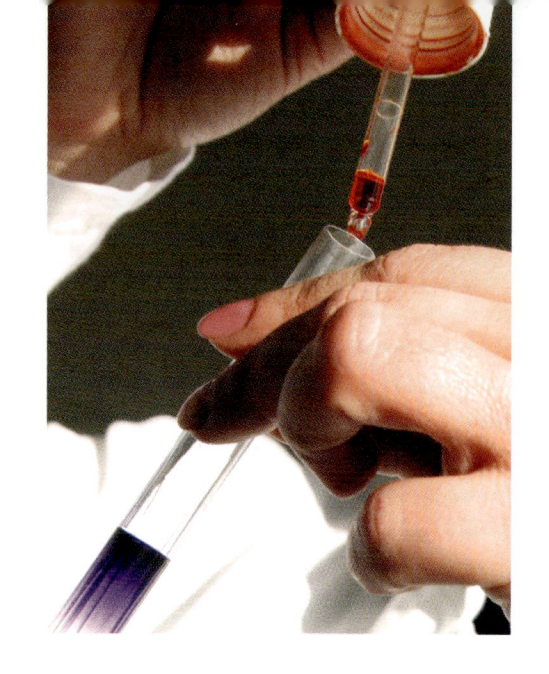

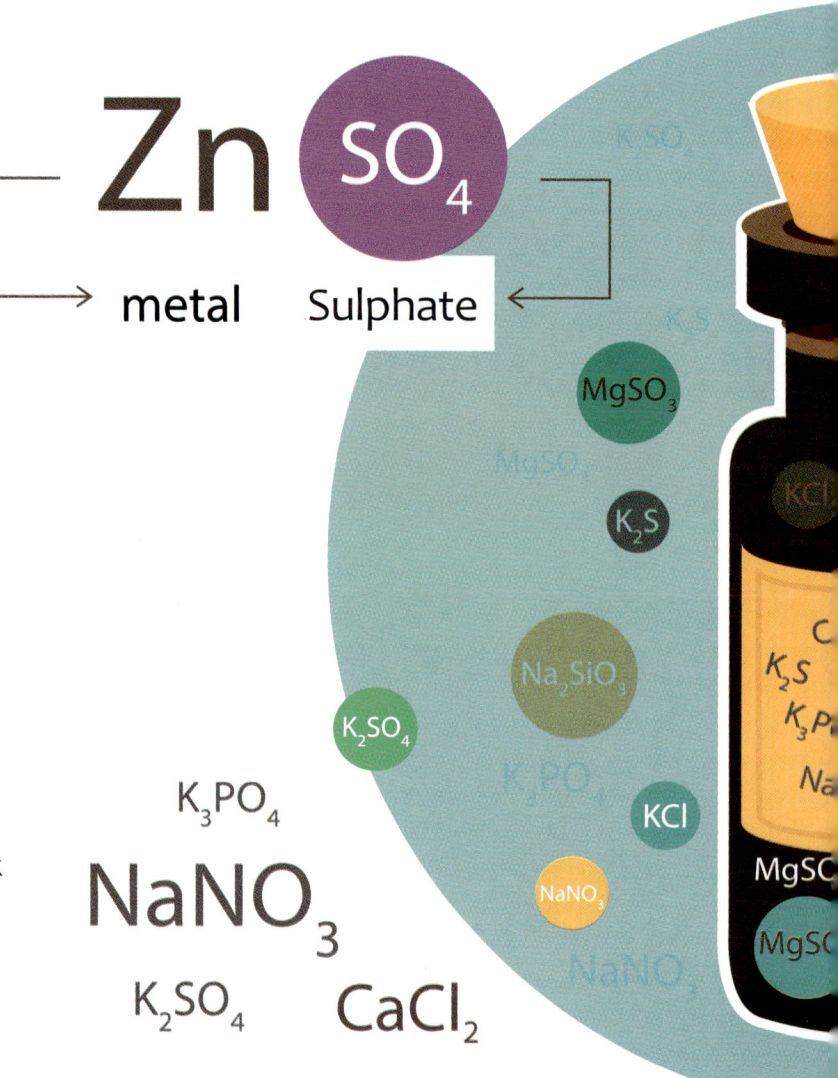

Zn SO_4
metal   Sulphate

$MgSO_3$
K_2S
Na_2SiO_3
K_2SO_4
K_3PO_4
$NaNO_3$
K_2SO_4 $CaCl_2$
KCl

30

SUBSTANCES, MIXTURES AND COMPOUNDS

Salts formed from acid–base reactions

The reaction of acids and bases form other salts, such as sodium bisulphate, potassium dichromate and calcium chloride. While all acid and base reactions form "salts", they are not all edible.

Calcium chloride

Calcium chloride is mainly used to remove the dampness in a room. It is marketed in the form of pellets. When used, it tends to absorb the moisture and water in the air. It reacts with this water and dissolves in it to leave behind a solution.

FUN FACT

When people accidentally swallow acidic liquids like bleach, they are made to drink baking powder solution so that it reacts with the acid, creating salt and water, causing them to throw up.

SCIENCE ENCYCLOPEDIA

Sodium bisulphate (NaHSO4)

Sodium bisulphate, along with potassium dichromate ($K_2Cr_2O_7$), is used as a bleach for photographic lenses and cameras. It reacts very badly with the skin so while handling this salt, people make sure to wear gloves and other bodily protection. It is also used as poison as it reacts very strongly when consumed.

Sample of calcium chloride.

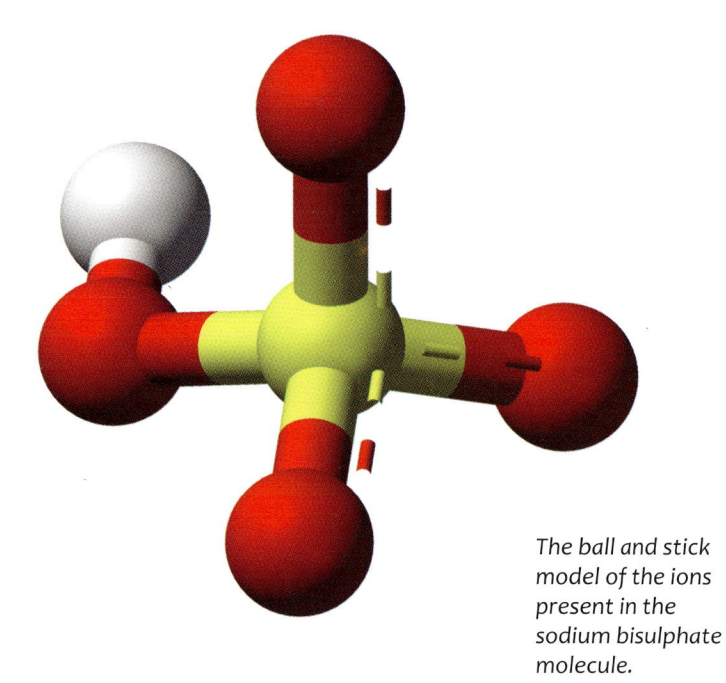

The ball and stick model of the ions present in the sodium bisulphate molecule.

Crystal salt

Sodium chloride (NaCl)

Common salt or table salt is the common name of sodium chloride. We use this salt in cooking. It is formed by the reaction of hydrochloric acid with the base, sodium hydroxide. This reaction is written as:

HCl + NaOH = H_2O + NaCl

(acid) (base) (water) (salt).

Sodium chloride is also found in a mineral called "halite" and hence is also called "rock salt". Particles of this salt exist in cubic crystals, which form a cubic lattice pattern. The bonds between the sodium and chloride atoms of this salt are one of the most basic and common examples of ionic bonding.

Carbon dioxide in the breath turns limewater milky.